Creating Classroom Structure

a practical guide for the special educator

Thomas Armstrong, MEd

SPECIAL CHILD PUBLICATIONS / SEATTLE

Special Child Publications
J. B. Preston, Editor & Publisher
P. O. Box 33548
Seattle, Washington 98133

Serving the special child since 1962

International Standard Book Number: 0-87562-081-7

93 92 91 90 89 88 87 86 85 84
10   9   8   7   6   5   4   3   2   1

Contents

Chapter 1
What You Are Going to Teach 5

Chapter 2
Who Needs to Learn What You Teach 27

Chapter 3
**How You Are Going to Teach What Your Students
        Need to Learn** 47

Chapter 4
**Where You Are Going to Keep Track of Who
        Has Learned What** 63

Chapter 5
When You Have Put It All Together 77

Afterword
Beyond Classroom Structure 79

Appendix
Selected Resources 83

The Author 93

Dedication

To Jason, Mat, Holly, Jamie, Bobby, Scottie, Darrell, Ronell, Joey, Melvin, Rachel, Ricky, Julia, Sheila, Stephen, Jennie, Mike, Donald, Robbie, Gina, Doug, Michael, Joanna, Don, Karl, Scott, Jackie, Larry, Shawn, Timmy, Steven, Lance, Jimmy, Kenny, Damion, and Betty.

Your lives have given this work its meaning and purpose.

What You Are Going To Teach
Defining the Limits of Your Unique Teaching Situation

The job of being a special educator has never been so complex. If your situation is typical, you must be familiar with a wide range of programs, techniques, assessment tools, interventions, child development theories, instructional materials, and sequential skills. As a special educator, you are expected to be a skill-based technician, a behavioral engineer, a personal growth facilitator, a perceptual psychologist, a reading specialist, a math expert, and an all-around super teacher and/or administrator. You are required to keep up with the tremendous influx of new information which has emerged during the past fifteen years in the field of special education. You need to know where you stand in the midst of widely differing philosophies, principles, and theories. You have to deal with the varied and sometimes erratic and conflicting expectations placed on you by administrators, parents, other teachers, students, yourself, and the law. You are faced with masses of paperwork in the course of assessing needs, developing educational plans, and creating instructional programs for each child you serve. You are faced with dwindling funds which require from you an even greater resourcefulness to see that inexpensive materials and methods are found which will meet each specific need.

To meet these demands requires that as a special educator, you develop efficient ways of assessing special needs, writing instructional goals, and creating appropriate instructional approaches to meet those needs; moreover, you need to develop some sort of overall system with which to organize and coordinate the many things which you must do in the course of meeting the current special education laws.

In response to these overwhelming demands, special educators have moved toward greater efficiency in their educational processing of children. This has resulted in the creation of commercially available, streamlined, multifunctioned programs designed to diagnose, prescribe, and "treat" every aspect of the child's psychoeducational program needs. Some school systems have gone so far as to run programs based primarily on computer print-outs of individual children's educational plans. Somehow in this search for greater efficiency, there is a danger that the more basic, human needs of both teacher and child will be left out. Each child is a unique individual, and can neither be reduced to a series of computer data sheets nor become a nameless cog in a comprehensive diagnostic-prescriptive learning program. So too, the teacher is much more than simply a manager of data or an engineer of treatments and interventions.

This book addresses the need for *both* humanism and efficiency. It is a book wherein educators can be empowered to create their own unique programs for each unique child, based on the individual life contexts of both teacher and child. At the same time, it provides the means through which an all-embracing structure can be created which will enable this humanizing process to take place.

This book is an aid to you, the special educator, in putting all of the complex elements of your profession together in a flexible program which reflects your personal style as an educator, and which can be adapted to the learning needs of any child or group of children you might work with. This book will help you to:

— Determine the scope of your particular job situation by defining the learning areas you are responsible for;
— Develop skills which are appropriate for each learning area;

- Find and use assessment tools with which to evaluate each skill;
- Establish criterion levels for each skill;
- Write specific instructional goals;
- Take inventory of your own present teaching resources;
- Create teaching approaches for each skill;
- Build your own reference file of skills, assessment tools, goals, and teaching approaches, which can be added to or modified over time; and
- Keep clear, efficient records of individual and group progress.

It is hoped that this book will not only serve as a blueprint for you in building your own program, but will allow you to look at the processes you use in going about the many complex tasks which constitute your role as a special educator.

Defining Your Limits

As a special education teacher, you must be prepared to encounter a wide range of needs from the children you deal with in your job; however, there are limits to which of those needs can be met in the classroom. Before the year has begun, you must determine the general nature of the needs you are likely to encounter during the year, and which of those needs you will be able to provide for. If you did not go through this process of limit-setting in some form, the task of preparation for your job would be awesome. You would have to prepare yourself for the possibility of encountering any sort of human need and providing for it in some way. Such a task is clearly impossible, however laudable. There are definite limits to those needs you can be responsible for. These limits are defined in part by the law, your professional training, your particular job situation, the expectations of those involved with your program, and your personal attitudes. Some of these limits are explicit, while others are only implied. What follows is a process which will help you to take a look at your responsibilities in a way that will allow you to determine, before the year has begun, the general limits of your job. Knowing the areas you will be responsible for ahead of time can save you problems later on in the year. It can enable you, in good conscience, to channel needs which are not within the scope of your job to appropriate personnel. It can also allow you to begin the task of developing a program for one or more of those areas, using the elements contained in this book.

Looking at the Universe of Skills

The range of human needs and the possibilities for what could be taught in an educational setting are ultimately as broad as the scope of human knowledge itself. In your own work, however, you need to be able to narrow things down considerably, since you very probably have neither the time, nor the inclinations or background to transmit the total fund of human knowledge to your students! For the purposes of this book, then, the concept of "skill" has been chosen as a way of structuring knowledge. The notion of "skill" has been selected both because it is a widely used concept in special education and because it allows educators to speak in terms of concrete, specific, and potentially useful units of knowledge in relation to the growing competence of the child. The term is used generically to identify categories of experience which have typically been used as units of instructional knowledge in schools, clinics, and other educational institutions. In using the term "skill," however, several things must be kept in mind. First, the list of skills which is to follow is far from exhaustive; second, skills function within the context of everyday life not as discrete entities, but in complex interactions with each other and with the child; and third, there is a considerable variation in the nature and scope of the skills which are listed on the following pages. Some deal purely with the dissemination of factual information; others deal with complex, multidimensional experience; still others are concerned primarily with the cultivation of inner qualities.

With all of this in mind, a "universe of skills" has been designed below, which attempts to encompas a broad range of instructional concerns within its framework.

This "universe of skills" is divided into five categories:

1. *Basic academic skills*—skills addressed in the "back-to-basics" movement: reading, writing, and arithmetic, as well as specific procedural skills which are required for success in an academic setting (e.g., reference skills, test-taking skills, etc.).
2. *Human processing skills*—skills governing basic human processes such as speaking, moving, thinking, and perceiving. These skills are dealt with more often in a clinical than an academic setting.*
3. *Practical life skills*—skills of application which usually involve some kind of real-life context for their development and attainment, such as tying one's shoe laces or cooking a meal.
4. *Behavioral/affective/social skills*—skills which deal with the complex and sometimes mysterious domain of human behavior, from specific behavioral objectives to more subjective areas such as self-concept development, social attitudes, and creativity.
5. *Content/knowledge skills*—these are the traditional content-based skill areas of school, such as knowledge of places, names, dates, facts, as well as generalized knowledge of ideas, theories, and principles in science, history, art, etc.

There is considerable overlap between the categories. Student problems in basic academic or practical life skills can often be traced to underlying difficulties in one or more of the human processing skills. Success in basic academic skills is required before specific content areas can be mastered or certain practical skills can be performed. Behavioral and affective skills can influence all other skill areas insofar as inappropriate behavior, low self-concept, or interpersonal conflict can function as obstacles to learning skills

---

*Although I dislike using human processing skills as a basis for program development in special education contexts, I include the category here because it is widely used. For a critique that, in part, outlines my views, see Lester Mann, "Psychometric Phrenology and the New Faculty Psychology: The Case Against Ability Assessment and Training," *Journal of Special Education* 5:1(1971) pp. 3-14, and Lester Mann, *On the Trail of Process: A Historical Perspective on Cognitive Processes and Their Training.* New York: Grune & Stratton, 1979.

in any of the other categories. By focusing on a particular area, one can also be reinforcing one or more areas in other categories. For example, in working on certain human processing skills, one can indirectly enhance basic academic skills, which can lead to greater knowledge of given content areas.

What follows is a listing of learning areas within each category, which could possibly form part of your instructional program. It is a lengthy but by no means exhaustive list of the possibilities. You might well discover learning areas of importance outside of this list, and you are encouraged to find them and use them in creating your program. Within each category are terms which might be considered to be repetitive in representing the same skills—for example, self-help skills and daily living skills. Similar terms have been included because certain labels may have a particular significance that you can immediately associate with a battery of skills; whereas other terms may be empty of personal meaning for you.

FIGURE 1.1. *The Universe of Skills.*

Basic academic skills
 Reading
  readiness
  decoding/word attack
  comprehension
  vocabulary
 Writing
  handwriting
  creative writing
  mechanics
  spelling
 Mathematics
  number theory
  computation
  problem solving
  logic
  geometry
  practical math
  higher mathematics

Test-taking
Study skills
Reference skills

Human processing skills
Perceptual channels
visual
auditory
tactile
kinesthetic
Perceptual-motor channels
gross-motor
fine-motor
Cross-modal/multisensory channels
Spatial orientation
Temporal orientation
Body concept/image/awareness
Cognitive styles/strategies
Psycholinguistics

Practical life skills
Self-help
Survival
Independent living
Family life
Prevocational and vocational
Career development
Job preparation
Shop
Homemaking
Recreation
Personal health/hygiene
Physical fitness
Consumer awareness
Business education
Technical education
Artistic education
Nutrition awareness
Civic education
Community adjustment
Financial management
Personal organization

Self-government
Mobility instruction
Human sexuality
Drug education

Behavioral/affective/social skills
Interpersonal communication
Group process
Self-concept
Personal growth
Moral development
Learning style development
Personality integration
Personal interests
Creativity development
Leadership
Human relations training
Will development
Intuition training
Imagination development
Social adjustment
Practical judgment
Conflict resolution
Problem-solving
Stress reduction

Content/knowledge skills
Traditional content-based academic subjects
art
math
science
history
literature
geography
social studies
music theory
government
foreign languages
Knowledge of specific instructional media
textbooks
workbooks
learning programs

books, magazines
multimedia (film, videotapes)
computer technology
Knowledge of designated subjects, fields, areas, or skills
Personal data
General fund of knowledge
Common sense information
Current events

You can select those terms from this list which have meaning for you and represent areas that you will be responsible for in your teaching.

Listing Others' Expectations
of What You're Going to Teach

You need to have some sort of criterion by which to decide what your educational limits are going to be. You can probably select many of the areas you plan to deal with in your job simply on the basis of past experience, a knowledge of your job description, an understanding of special education laws as they apply to you, and an intuitive sense of what is expected of you in your work. If you wish, you can make a quick list from the "universe of skills" and proceed directly to the next section, where you will develop skills for each of the areas you have selected; or, you can fill out the worksheet on the following page, which will help you to:

1. Gain more insight into the processes you use in deciding what you will teach;
2. Obtain information on the kinds of expectations which other personnel have for you as an educator;
3. Give priority to those teaching areas which you deem most important within the scope of your teaching duties; and
4. Emphasize those teaching areas in which professional development is most urgently required.

Areas of need based on kind of children in program	Expectations of others	Areas I feel most qualified for or enjoy teaching

FIGURE 1.2. *Priorities Worksheet.*

Areas I want or need to be responsible for but for which I do not feel qualified at present	Areas I feel responsible for but do not wish to teach	Areas I plan to be responsible for during the year

Each of the headings in this worksheet provides information which can be helpful to you in defining your job:

Areas of need based on kind of children in program. This column represents the program needs based upon information about the kind of children who will be served. Such information may come from:

1. Individualized educational plans (IEPs)* of each child;
2. Evaluations by team members either before or after the IEP has been written;
3. Cumulative records in school files; or
4. Other formal or informal reports, observations, anecdotal information, previous program records, etc.

If complete assessments and IEPs have not yet been completed on all the students you will be responsible for, then your knowledge of which skill areas are relevant to your job situation might be incomplete until further information is supplied. You are not necessarily going to be responsible for all areas of need indicated by these assessments, of course. The IEP, your job description, and the roles of other personnel—as well as other factors indicated in following pages—will determine the areas you will be primarily responsible for, and which areas will be covered by other support personnel. Once this list has been completed, you can sit down with all school personnel who will be responsible for the children in your program, and jointly decide on who is going to be primarily responsible for assessing and teaching in each skill area. Such a meeting is important to the team process. In the course of writing IEPs, specific information needs to be supplied on most forms concerning who is to assume the responsibility for different parts of the plan. While the division of labor in a school setting is often implicit upon entering a new job situation, ironing out beforehand which personnel will be responsible for given areas can avoid time-wasting discussions during

---

*The term, IEP, as used here and throughout the book, refers to any formal evaluation plan drawn up by an educational institution for the purposes of meeting a child's educational needs. This term may not be relevant to your individual teaching situation, however, in which case it can be passed over in your reading of the book.

IEP meetings, duplication of effort, and conflicts and gaps in serving children's needs. Some time spent at the beginning of the school year reviewing the standards and precedents of your school or district may be helpful.

Expectations of others. In this column, list those areas which you feel others expect you to deal with in your teaching. These expectations may be explicit, in terms of a specific job description, a program which you are expected to follow, or specific IEP goals; or they may be implied, based on what you know of the parties involved from past experience with them. Except for expectations which you feel are generally shared by all parties in the educational process, indicate the particular party connected with each expectation (parents, administrators, teachers, team members, children, etc.). State specific individuals, if necessary. Filling out this column will make clear possible areas of conflict which can then be dealt with. If the expectations of others do not match the expectations which you have for yourself—as noted in the following three columns—then there is a need for communication between the parties involved to determine exactly what your role will be. By communicating with the other parties to the process, you may discover their expectations were different from what you had thought. Particularly with parents and children, you may be able to clear up misconceptions they might have had about your role. With coworkers, you can work out creative solutions to potential areas of conflict. This particular need will be discussed further in the following pages.

Areas I feel most qualified for, or enjoy teaching. In this column, list skill areas in which you have special training, which you have enjoyed teaching in the past, or which you have never taught but would enjoy teaching if given an opportunity. You needn't restrict yourself in this column only to areas which seem applicable to your own teaching situation. This column represents an opportunity to take a look at some of the things in teaching that really "turn you on," or that you really do well. Later on, in the final column of this worksheet, you will be given the chance to look over the areas you have chosen here and decide which ones could become a part of your duties and responsibilities as a teacher.

Areas I want or need to be responsible for, but for which I do not feel qualified at present. You probably have a clear sense, even before doing this worksheet, of skill areas which you do not feel qualified for or do not feel prepared yet to teach. It might be that you have found yourself inheriting a job description which contains elements that were not a part of your teacher training program, previous teaching experience, or inservice training; or, you may feel that your training or experience, while appropriate to a given area, still leaves you short of where you'd like to be in feeling confident with that group of skills. Completing this column will give you a better sense of the gaps that exist between your professional expertise and your program demands. You can then pursue any number of options to close that gap and meet your needs as an educator. Among those options, you can:

1. Make provisions for appropriate training:
   a. inservice training
   b. workshops, courses, lectures
   c. individual reading, research, and study
   d. contact with appropriate personnel or outside experts
   e. professional support groups
2. Negotiate with school personnel to:
   a. modify job description
   b. transfer responsibility for a given area to other school personnel
   c. share responsibility for a given skill area with other personnel more experienced in that area.

In addition, the process of going through this book and developing specific skills, assessment tools, instructional goals, and teaching methods for those areas you feel deficient in, will help a great deal in fulfilling your own professional needs as well.

Areas I feel responsible for, but do not wish to teach. This column is perhaps the most difficult to complete. Here, you are to list areas which you feel you will have to deal with in the course of your teaching, but do not wish to teach. This may be the case for any number of reasons. You may not feel qualified to teach a particular area, in which case you should find it listed in the previous column and deal with it as suggested in the preceding section. You may feel pressured by your colleagues into dealing with it—note which areas you have listed in the "expectations" column—and experience resentment or anger at having to do this. You may feel temperamentally unsuited to deal with a particular group of skills, or have philosophical or theoretical objections to teaching certain areas. You may simply dislike a certain area (for example, some of those in the "content/knowledge" area) because it was presented ineffectively to you as a child in school, or simply because you experience the area as dull, uninteresting, and not worth your effort in teaching. If any of these reasons apply, it is important to talk with your professional colleagues about your feelings concerning those areas you feel resistant to teaching. Otherwise, you might experience stress and frustration when dealing with those areas. This stress can then be communicated in some way to your students. Or, you might find subtle ways to avoid dealing with the offending areas and thereby deprive your pupils of needed services. Communicating your feelings to your supervisor and others with whom you work professionally can lead to a solution. You may not have to deal with the area after all. You may be able to achieve a compromise in the way that you approach a particular area. Communicating with colleagues who are experienced in those areas you are concerned about may change your own attitudes and feelings about teaching them. In any case, sharing feelings with colleagues about this and any other problems which occur in the process of serving your students is a *must* to ensure the success of any educational program.

Areas I plan to be responsible for during the year. After having completed the first five columns, you are ready to make final choices about the areas to which you will commit yourself during the year. These will be the areas that you can take on through this book and develop into an instructional program for yourself. Before making these final choices, you may need to consult with all the parties to the IEP process to be clear about their expectations and your own feelings about the areas for which your particular job makes you responsible. After making your choices, arrange them in terms of which areas you would most like to put into your instructional program. You may wish to structure an area of strength and familiarity into your program; or, you might want to focus on areas of need for your own professional development. Even if you are not yet clear on all of the areas which will define your teaching role during the school year, you can still take one or more areas which are priorities for you and build a program around them. As a start, the skill area which receives the highest priority for you can be taken into the subsequent sections of this book and can be developed, step by step, into a workable program.

Determining the Skills You Are Going to Teach within Each Area

Once you have chosen the areas you are going to be responsible for in your teaching, you are ready to begin the task of building an instructional program. As a first step, you need to determine the group of specific skills which will form the substance of each area you have chosen to work with. There are several factors to consider in choosing skills for a given area:

1. How are the skills to be organized? Some areas will require skills to be highly sequential (e.g., computational math or the learning of a complex practical task). Other areas will involve nonsequential but interdependent skills (as in the affective area, where—for example—self-esteem can lead to improved social cooperation and vice versa). Finally, some areas will involve nonsequential skills where little consideration need be paid to how they are organized in relation to each other.

2. In what kind of educational setting are the skills to be applied? What are the grade levels, ages, or developmental ranges of the students in the program? The range of skills involved in a math program will vary considerably from a kindergarten through third-grade setting of hearing-impaired youngsters, to a high school population of developmentally delayed students. The broader the developmental levels and learning needs you are addressing, the wider the spectrum of skills you will need to develop.

3. What kind of priority do I place on each skill area in terms of the students' needs? If you are teaching students who are visually impaired, then you will probably construct a wider range of independent living skills, than would the person who is working with a group of students in a resource room program who wishes to include this area as a supplementary part of a primarily academic program.

It's important to emphasize at this point that you needn't create a whole battery of skills the first time around. You may just want to begin a skeleton structure of skills around a particular area; and then, once you begin working with the children and attending to particular situations, you can write in skills which emerge from your assessment of each child's needs. This is a great way to preserve your efforts as you write IEPs. Taking skills which have emerged from one child's plan, you can make them a permanent part of your program to draw upon in the future when similar needs are encountered.

There are many resources available from which to select the skills you will need to start your program:

1. Commercially available programs and materials provide well-organized packages of skills in many areas. You may, of course, decide that certain programs do a far better job of meeting a child's needs than you could ever put together on your own. If so, then you can choose to use these programs in their entirety and concentrate only on those areas where comprehensive programs are not available or are not constructed to suit your particular teaching needs. You might also choose to use part of a commercial program and then supplement it with skills from your own self-created program to fill in gaps you may feel to exist in the commercial program; or, you can simply use these programs as models of how skills and programs can be organized. Many commercial programs which have been recently published, are constructed to be within present education law; and they contain precisely worded skills and objectives which can be

a help in generating ideas and guidance for your own personalized program. Look for these programs in your school's resource center, district curriculum library, county or regional instructional centers, or order information on them from special education commercial catalogs. (See Appendix.) Manufacturers and publishers will often send you a complimentary booklet or summary of their programs which contains listings of the skills covered in the programs. This can give you ideas on which skills to include in your own program.

2. Individual schools and school districts have created programs in many skill areas which can be used as guides. The programs often have skills checklists or articulation cards which are easily available; and they list specific skills for each area, particularly in the basic academic skills and content/knowledge categories. Vocational schools and programs could provide skills relating to many practical life skill areas. Clinical programs might provide programs relating to human processing and behavioral/affective/social skill areas.

3. Talk to those knowledgeable in the areas for which you seek skill-related information: department heads, curriculum specialists, administrators of relevant programs, and special educators who are proficient in the areas for which you are seeking help. Seek out creative teachers who have constructed their own programs and have refined them over the course of years. Discover from them how they have defined and organized their skills in each area that concerns you.

4. Textbooks, professional books, and other published materials which deal with the areas you are working on, can provide information you can use in defining your skills. Of particular value would be ERIC, the computerized educational research network which includes descriptions of numerous programs in all areas listed in the "universe of skills" section; also, consult *Exceptional Child Abstracts.*

5. Alternative schools, private school programs, spe-

cial education clinics, hospitals' education departments, professional mental health agencies, adult education programs, and other relevant agencies have often developed their own programs that are competency-based and list skills that can help you create your own program.

6. Other sources include state boards of education, which can provide valuable information concerning state proficiency requirements for graduation from high school; county or regional programs, which are setting up computerized data banks of skills to help facilitate the writing of instructional goals in school districts; and finally, one's own personal experience, expertise, and common sense of what skills would be appropriate to each area chosen.

Once you have determined an initial group of relevant skills for a given skill area, you are ready to begin completing the instructional program sheets which are to serve as the framework for your program. This simple form, when completed, will provide all of the information necessary for you to assess for each specific skill, establish criterion levels, write specific instructional goals, and select appropriate teaching methods to match the skills being taught.

Definition of terms used in the instructional program sheet.

1. *Skill area*—major groups taken from the universe of skills (basic academic skills, practical life skills, etc.);
2. *Skills*—the skills which belong to each area (handwriting, vocabulary, geometry, etc.);
3. *Assessments*—the particular tools which you are going to use to determine whether or not the child possesses that particular skill;
4. *Criteria*—the level(s) of mastery or proficiency which must be reached in order for a skill to have been learned and/or applied;
5. *Goals*—the specific instructional objectives for each skill which can be written into the child's IEP; and
6. *Teaching approaches*—the variety of teaching methods, materials, and strategies for each skill (items which are accessible to you and appropriate to the child's needs). See Figure 1.3, following.

FIGURE 1.3. Instructional Program Sheet with First Column Completed.

Skills	Assessments	Criteria	Goals	Approaches
Able to compute basic addition facts — on sums to 10 — on sums to 18				
Able to compute addition problems of — 2 digits plus 2 digits with no regrouping — 3 digits plus 3 digits with no regrouping				

— 2 digits plus
2 digits with re-
grouping
— 3 digits plus
3 digits with 2
regroupings

Able to add col-
umns of
— 3 one-digit
numbers
— columns of 5
two-digit num-
bers

Chapter 2

Who Needs to Learn What You Teach
Defining the Limits of Each Student's Unique Learning Situation

Selecting the Tools You Are Going to Use to Assess for Each Skill

Once you have begun the process of selecting skills and listing them on the instructional program sheet, your next step involves developing ways to assess the extent to which each skill has been mastered or learned. Prior development of assessment tools for skills which are relevant to your teaching situation will enable you to evaluate students effectively in several ways:

1. The tools can be used in initial assessments of children to determine their general area of need. This will provide useful information in the development of their IEPs.

2. Once general areas of need have been established and basic goals have been developed for the child as a part of the IEP, assessment tools can be used to create specific instructional goals.

3. After the IEP has been completed, with specific goals having been written and the process of teaching having begun, the assessment tools can be used as a means of evaluating progress toward specific

goals and determining the point at which goals are met.

4. Assessment tools can be used to affirm or validate the mastery of skills in areas of strength for each child and thereby develop a sense of competence and proficiency in the student when this information is reported back to him.

The kinds of tools you can use for assessment purposes include:

1. Commercially available assessment materials of all kinds, such as:
    a. standardized achievement tests
    b. intelligence tests
    c. criterion-referenced tests
    d. oral and silent reading tests and inventories
    e. projective tests
    f. scales and continuums
    g. perceptual assessments
2. Checklists
3. Observations/anecdotes/teacher journal
4. Dittos and worksheets from commercial programs
5. Teacher-made dittos
6. Practical situations, performance tests
7. Games, puzzles, novel situations
8. Simulations
9. Concrete materials of all kinds, such as:
    a. building materials
    b. art equipment
    c. musical instruments
10. Media such as:
    a. films
    b. pictures
    c. recordings
11. Dialogue and discussion
12. Paper-and-pencil tests
13. Chalkboard exams
14. Books, textbooks, magazines, reference material
15. Samples of students' work, such as:
    a. writing samples
    b. student projects

      c. pictures or recordings of work

      d. student journals or other self-evaluations

16. Graphs and charts of performance or behavior

The kinds of tools you select for each skill will depend on a variety of factors:

1. *Number of people to whom the tool is administered.* Will you give the assessment individually, in small groups, or to large classes?

2. *Developmental level and learning style of each student.* Does the student need concrete materials, or is he or she able to handle the skill on a more abstract level, using pencil and paper, question and answer, chalkboard, etc.?

3. *Length of assessment.* Do you want a quick assessment, or a more thorough examination of the factors involved in the students' acquisition of skill?

4. *Budget.* Do you have money available to purchase commercial assessment instruments? Do you have access to a variety of commercial and/or teacher-made assessment tools, or are you going to have to develop many of them on your own?

5. *Type of skill.* Are you assessing:
   a. behavioral or practical skills requiring the student to apply something to real life?
   b. processing skills requiring the student to demonstrate inner processes of thinking or perceiving?
   c. subjective skills requiring the student to demonstrate qualitative characteristics?

6. *Learning channels.* Do you want tools which:
   a. require primarily auditory or visual functioning?
   b. involve cross-modal experiences?
   c. require precise fine-motor abilities?

An assessment tool which capitalizes on a child's strongest learning channels will increase the validity of the results.

For any given skill, a variety of methods are possible to assess the skill. For example, if you wish to find out whether a student is able to add different combinations of two numbers to a sum of 18, you could:

1. Use a commercially available program which con-

tains a section on addition of numbers with sums to 18.

2. Use a test or a worksheet from a kindergarten through third-grade program which consists of addition problems up to sums of 18.

3. Use a teacher-made test using a ditto on which are written several addition problems with sums to 18.

4. Have the child go up to the chalkboard and give the student several problems in succession with sums to 18, and note the process the student uses in solving the problems. (Does the pupil count on fingers, count aloud, erase a lot, etc.?)

5. Give the child some concrete manipulatives (beans, shells, blocks, etc.), and have the student add different combinations together.

6. Quiz the child orally on knowledge of addition facts on sums to 18.

7. Show the child flashcards of different addition combinations, and have the student say or write the answers.

8. Tell the child word problems based on the student's own experience and interests (comics, candy, money, etc.) which require adding combinations of numbers up to 18.

9. Have another student in class quiz the child on addition problems to 18, and observe the administration.

10. Have the child write or recite the addition tables of $1 + 1 = 2$, etc., up to $9 + 9 = 18$, in rhythm to music.

Of course, you would probably not want to list 10 or 15 assessment tools for each specific skill in your program! But you can choose, if possible, two or more tools for each skill, which would allow you some flexibility in meeting different kinds of needs. This way, if a child with hearing problems, for example, is to be assessed in computational math, he will not have to be subjected to an oral quiz in order to determine his competence in arithmetic. Or, if you work both with individuals and small groups, you would have the flexibility to assess groups on a skill or do an individual assessment. Again, it will depend upon the kind of job you have, your duties and responsibilities, the sort of children you serve, the organization of the program, etc. The broader the responsibilities you have and the wider the range of children you serve, the more varied should be the kinds of assessment resources you should build into your program.

In order to determine which tools to include on the instructional program sheet under assessments, make an inventory of all the assessment tools that you presently have available to you in those areas you have selected to create in your instructional program. Then, go through the list of skills which you have created and write in the tools you already have under the "assessments" column of the instructional program sheet next to each relevant skill. The program sheet should then look something like the sample shown on the next page. When you have finished this process, make a note of those skills for which you have not listed any means of assessment. For these skills, you must generate a means of assessment from somewhere. It might involve:

1. Ordering materials;
2. Visiting the diagnostic center in your district, or your school's center, for available materials;
3. Obtaining materials from educational programs in other classes, schools, curriculum departments;
4. Creating your own teacher-made equipment, materials, or informal assessments.

Selecting the right assessment tools for your program involves a process of continual refinement or development over a period of time which occurs alongside of your own professional development as a special educator. You may not be required to deal with a particular skill or group of skills which you have listed in your program, until you encounter a specific child whose needs require that skill. Then you will have information about the child which will enable you to determine what kind of assessment tool would best serve the interests and needs of that child. When you have done this, you have not only met the needs of an individual child, but you have also added what you have learned from the case to your personal resource structure—the instructional program you are creating—where it will continue to serve you in the future.

FIGURE 2.1. *Instructional Program Sheet with Second Column Completed.*

Skills	Assessments	Criteria	Goals	Approaches
Able to compute basic addition facts — on sums to 10 — on sums to 18	1. chalkboard exam; note strategy used 2. teacher-made ditto 3. oral quiz 4. peer given flash cards			
Able to compute addition problems of — 2 digits plus 2 digits with no regrouping	1. teacher-made skill card 2. dittoed worksheet page			
— 3 digits plus 3 digits with no regrouping	1. teacher-made skill card 2. dittoed work-			

— 2 digits plus
2 digits with re-
grouping
— 3 digits plus
3 digits with 2
regroupings

sheet page
1. teacher-made
skill card
2. dittoed work-
sheet page
3. abacus; note
strategy when re-
grouping

Able to add col-
umns of
— 3 one-digit
numbers
— columns of 5
two-digit num-
bers

1. chalkboard ex-
am; note strategy
used
2. teacher-made
ditto
3. beans as count-
ers; note how
uses

Organizing Your Assessment Resources

Once you have listed and gathered together the assessment tools you will use during the year, you need to organize those materials so that they can be quickly found and used as the need arises. For this purpose, a filing drawer or file box can be used to house tests, checklists, worksheets, and other paper materials which will be used in assessing each skill. They can be filed according to specific skill or by skill area, depending on the number of assessments you will be using. Some examples of what might be included in an assessment file are presented here from each of the five basic categories of the universe of skills.

Category: Basic Academic Skills
Area: reading/phonics
Contents of Assessment File:
— list of nonsense words
— several phonics worksheets from workbooks
— a pack of phoneme cards
— a commercial test for group diagnosis of phonetic difficulties

Category: Human Processing Skills
Area: auditory perception
Contents of Assessment File:
— auditory discrimination test
— list of number and word sequences to be repeated
— a tape recording, testing auditory figure-ground skills
— a list of oral directions to be carried out by the student
— a fairytale to be read and then "told back" to the teacher

Category: Practical Life Skills
Area: consumer awareness
Contents of Assessment File:
— labels from food cans and food ads with a teacher-made ditto asking questions requiring comparison shopping skills
— a questionnaire concerning personal consumer attitudes
— a consumer math test of weights and measures
— several order forms from commercial catalogs

Category: Behavioral/Affective/Social Skills
Area: self-concept
Contents of Assessment File:
— a checklist of factors for teacher observation
— a self-report inventory
— a rating scale
— a sheet listing informal assessment of draw-a-person activities
— a list of self-concept activities to use for assessment purposes

Category: Content/Knowledge Skills
Area: science
Contents of Assessment File:
— pop quizzes, midterms, and final exam
— requirements for science projects
— checklist of science interests
— college preparatory achievement test

Concrete materials which will not fit in a file can be kept as part of your regular teaching materials. If the materials are used primarily or solely for assessment purposes, they can be put in shoeboxes or other storage containers and then kept together as a group in a particular area of the room or in a certain closet. Commercial assessment kits could be included there, as well.

Setting Up Levels of Competence for Each Skill

Once you have established the skill and the means by which the skill is to be evaluated, a criterion needs to be established as a standard against which the student's own level of performance can be gauged. You need to determine what a student must know and/or do to enable you to say that he or she has acquired the particular skill being assessed. There are different ways of defining the concept of competence in skill learning, which depend upon the kind of skill, the means of assessment, and the philosophy of the teacher. There are, however, three basic ways to articulate a criterion:

1. *Quantitative.* The most common means of determining competence in skill learning is according to

numerically measurable standards. These can be expressed in different ways:

    a. a percentage (with 70 or 80 percent, or higher, often being considered a standard for the acquisition of a skill);

    b. a fraction (e.g., seven correct out of ten problems);

    c. a number which exists within the context of a given time frame (e.g., 50 push-ups in ten minutes); or

    d. a quantity of something (e.g., 20 positive self-statements).

2. *Functional.* Articulation of proficiency involves the performance of some specific behavior or series of behaviors, the components of which must be performed before the skill can be said to have been learned. This category is more likely to be of an all-or-nothing quality. Either the student knows how to do the particular skill, or he doesn't (e.g., tie shoes, dissect a frog, draw an angle with a compass and straight-edge, touch right hand to left toe, etc.). There can be several components, however, to a skill, with mastery being applied at each stage along the way (e.g., for tying a shoe—being able to thread a hole, thread a series of holes, tie a knot, a bow, etc.). Here, growing levels of competence can be measured as a fraction of the stages of the skill which have been mastered (e.g., three out of five components required for tying one's shoe).

3. *Qualitative.* This means of expressing mastery refers to those skills which need to be evaluated on the basis of subjective or phenomenological factors. Qualitative criteria are particularly relevant to the behavioral/affective/social skills category, for such areas as self-concept development, creativity, and social awareness—but are applicable to other areas as well. "Behavioral subjectives," as I prefer to call them, present a challenge for educators seeking to create valid measures of achievement and progress. They cannot be undervalued or neglected, because they involve many of the most vital concerns and needs of children with special needs. To be most useful and valid, qualitative cri-

teria should:

a. be expressed in clear, precise language, using concrete experience and behavioral language where possible;

b. use a variety of informal assessment procedures (e.g., well kept anecdotal records, inventories, student self-evaluations, student work, pictures, etc.);

c. involve more than one person in the evaluation if possible (e.g., teacher, parent, administrator, child, etc.).

When you are establishing criterion levels, there are several resources you can turn to for indications of which standards are considered most appropriate for each skill. This is particularly necessary for skills requiring quantitative measures of competence for which you want to establish a level of mastery which is neither too high nor too low for your purposes. These sources include:

1. Commercially available assessment programs or educational programs where criterion levels for skills are usually given;

2. Teachers and specialists experienced in their field, who have a good sense of what constitutes levels of mastery or competence in the skills which they have taught for years;

3. Your own sense of what levels of performance constitute mastery in a given skill, based upon your past experience and training in that field. Your own sense of mastery levels is particularly important, since it is *you* who best knows the particular children and learning situations in which the skill is to be acquired.

Remember that the children you serve needn't achieve a particular mastery level in order to have achieved a goal. You write the goal for them in terms of any level of achievement you feel would be appropriate to their ability and learning style. This may be far below, or even above, the specific level of mastery that is considered "standard." You could give a lower instructional level, or even lower so-called "frustration" level, and a high "overlearn" level in addition to the "standard" level of mastery. This would provide additional means of gauging a student's progress toward a given skill. Your goal for a student then might be to take him or her from a "frustration" level to an "instructional" level, where the student has not yet mastered a skill but is able to function in that skill without discouragement. If you wish to reinforce positive school achievement, for example, you can set the criterion level for that particular student above the basic mastery level. If the skill is a functional one, you can list the components of the skill in the "skill" section of the instructional program sheet, and then be able to evaluate progress in the skill according to how many of the components have been achieved. For the qualitative skills, the "criteria" section of the instructional program sheet could include a list of the factors to be considered in evaluating the mastery of the skill, the personnel to be responsible for evaluating, and how the assessment tools will be used to establish mastery (e.g., teacher journal notes will keep records of the student's positive self-statements). See the following figure for a sample of how the "criteria" section might be filled out on the instructional program sheet.

Writing Instructional Goals

Having already established the specific skills to be learned, the assessment tools to be used, and the criterion for mastery of the skill, you have already performed most of the work that you need to do in order to prepare for writing of instructional goals. Now all you have to do is to put these elements together in one concise verbal package, and your goal will be written. What follows are examples which have been taken from each of the five categories of the universe of skills, to illustrate how the three elements of skill, assessment tools, and criterion levels can be combined to establish a specific instructional goal.

Category: Basic Academic Skills
Area: reading
Skill: reading 250 basic sight words
Assessment tool: Dolch list of 250 basic sight words on flashcards (visual-oral learning channel).
Criterion: 240/250 sight words correctly read.
Goal: When presented with the Dolch list of 250 com-

mon sight words in the form of individual flashcards one at a time, the student will be able to orally read 240 of them to the examiner.

Category: Human Processing Skills
Area: auditory memory
Skill: to be able to repeat 7 digit numbers from short-term memory.
Assessment tool: a list of telephone numbers from a sample page of a local directory given orally to the student.
Criterion: Out of 10 seven-digit phone numbers, the student will correctly say 7 of the numbers with the digits in the proper order.
Goal: When the student is orally given 10 phone numbers of seven digits each from a sample page of a local phone directory, he/she will be able to orally repeat from memory each number after hearing it read, correctly repeating at least 7 out of the 10 phone numbers.

Category: Practical Life Skills
Area: independent living skills
Skill: to be able to cook a simple meal
Assessment tools: kitchen facilities, food ingredients, cooking utensils, recipe books, checklists of components to the process.
Criterion: Completion of each component to the process: lighting stove, finding recipes and ingredients, correctly measuring, mixing and cooking ingredients, setting table. Final product must include a main dish, a side vegetable, a grain or potato, a beverage and a dessert. Meal must be edible to a teacher.
Goal: Given proper kitchen facilities, food ingredients, cooking utensils, recipe books and other necessary equipment, the student will be able to complete all of the components to cooking a simple edible meal consisting of a main dish, a side vegetable, a grain or potato, a beverage and a dessert.

Category: Behavioral/Affective/Social Skills
Area: self-concept
Skill: to say positive self-statements

FIGURE 2.2. Instructional Program Sheet with Third Column Completed.

Skills	Assessments	Criteria	Goals	Approaches
Able to compute basic addition facts	1. chalkboard exam; note strategy used	100%		
— on sums to 10 — on sums to 18	2. teacher-made ditto 3. oral quiz 4. peer given flashcards	9 out of 10 problems given		
Able to compute addition problems of	1. teacher-made skill card			
— 2 digits plus 2 digits with no regrouping	2. dittoed worksheet page	70 - 90% de pending on student		
— 3 digits plus 3 digits with no regrouping	1. teacher-made skill card 2. dittoed work-	same as above		

– 2 digits plus 2 digits with re-grouping – 3 digits plus 3 digits with 2 regroupings	sheet page 1. teacher-made skill card 2. dittoed work-sheet page 3. abacus; note strategy when re-grouping	same as above same as above
Able to add columns of – 3 one-digit numbers – columns of 5 two-digit numbers	1. chalkboard exam; note strategy used 2. teacher-made ditto 3. beans as counters; note how uses	80% 70%

Assessment tool: teacher recording of self-statements made by student, written down in teacher anecdotal journal.

Criterion: an increase in the number of positive self-statements (such as, "I like this drawing I made," "I'm good at math," "I love the new shirt I have on").

Goal: The student will increase the incidence of positive self-statements (such as, "I'm good at math," "I like the drawing I made") from the present 3 times per week as recorded in the teacher's anecdotal journal, to 6 times per week.

Category: Content/Knowledge Skills
Area: American history
Skill: to be able to list the names of the 13 original American colonies.
Assessment tool: a piece of paper with 13 blanks, student requested orally to list in pencil on a piece of paper the 13 original American colonies.
Criterion: 12 out of 13 colonies within a 10 minute time period.
Goal: Given a pencil and a sheet of paper with 13 blanks and requested orally to write the names of the 13 original American colonies, the student will correctly write at least 12 of them within a period of 10 minutes.

Depending upon the particular assessment tool or criterion you use, your instructional goal is going to be expressed differently for the same skill. For example, if we take the last skill used as an example and apply a different assessment tool and a different criterion, we will come up with a different goal:

Category: Content/Knowledge Skills
Area: American history
Skill: to be able to list the names of the 13 original American colonies.
Assessment tool: oral quiz. The teacher will ask the student to orally recite from memory in any order the names of the 13 original colonies.
Criterion: 13 out of 13 colonies within a 3 minute time period (100%).

Goal: When requested to do so, the student will orally recite from memory in any order the names of all 13 original American colonies within a 3 minute time period.

To provide the needed flexibility when writing instructional goals onto the program sheet under the goals column, you can do several things:

1. Write one basic goal, but leave blanks for certain words or numbers which can be altered according to the particular criterion you have chosen to meet the individual needs of each child. For example: The student will increase in incidence of positive self-statements ("I'm good at math," "I like the drawing I made") from the present . . . times per . . . as recorded in the teacher's anecdotal journal to . . . times per . . . .

2. Write more than one goal for each skill to account for different assessment tools being used—as in the American history example.

3. Write one basic goal for each skill as a standard which can be reworded or rephrased when it is time to write it into a child's IEP.

4. Leave the goals column blank for skills which require a multiplicity of expressions and simply use the other data from the program sheet to write the appropriate goals as required.

Making provision for one or more of these suggestions builds into your program another degree of flexibility which allows you to respond to the needs of the moment, while at the same time having the structures of skills, assessment tools, criteria, and goals to draw upon in creating an educational program for each student. It is this balance of structure and flexibility which makes your program an invaluable aid in serving the needs of your students. It requires an initial investment of time, but once a basic structure has been started, you have a framework which will begin to serve you well in years ahead. The time you save by this initial organization will more than make up for the few days it took to put it all together!

The following page gives an example of how the program sheet might look after you have filled in the goals col-

FIGURE 2.3. Instructional Program Sheet with Fourth Column Completed.

Skills	Assessments	Criteria	Goals	Approaches
Able to compute basic addition facts — on sums to 10 — on sums to 18	1. chalkboard exam; note strategy used 2. teacher-made ditto 3. oral quiz 4. peer given flashcards	100% 9 out of 10 problems given	Given a teacher-made ditto of 10 addition problems with sums of . . . , the student will correctly solve . . . of the problems.	
Able to compute addition problems of — 2 digits plus 2 digits with no regrouping	1. teacher-made skill card 2. dittoed worksheet page	70 - 90% depending on student	Given a dittoed worksheet page of 10 problems involving . . . digit plus . . . digit addition without regroup, the student will solve . . . of them.	
— 3 digits plus 3 digits with no regrouping	1. teacher-made skill card 2. dittoed work-	same as above		

— 2 digits plus 2 digits with regrouping — 3 digits plus 3 digits with 2 regroupings	sheet page 1. teacher-made skill card 2. dittoed work-sheet page 3. abacus; note strategy when regrouping	same as above same as above	Given a teacher-made skill card of 10 problems involving . . . digit plus . . . digit addition with (1,2) regroupings, the student will solve . . . of them.
Able to add columns of — 3 one-digit numbers — columns of 5 two-digit numbers	1. chalkboard exam; note strategy used 2. teacher-made ditto 3. beans as counters; note how uses	80% 70%	Given 10 problems on the chalkboard involving column addition of (3,5) (1,2) digit numbers, the student will solve . . . of them.

umn for each skill. The processes and techniques of putting together a good instructional goal have only been briefly touched upon here. The reader is referred to several books which have come out recently on how to write instructional goals, which are excellent sources to help you continue this process of creating appropriate goals for your students. These references are found in the list of resources in the appendix.

Chapter 3

How You Are Going to Teach What Your Students Need to Learn

Defining and Developing Your Own Unique Constellation of Teaching Resources

The next step in putting it all together involves selecting the materials which you will employ in meeting the goals you have written for each skill. Before you can do this, you will want to take a look at what your present teaching resources are and how you can go about developing additional resources to meet the specific needs of the children in your program. You will want a system which will help integrate the vast amount of educational knowledge which has entered your awareness during your career. You will want to develop the means which will allow that material to filter most directly into your classroom teaching and bridge the gap between theory and practice.

We all do some of this intuitively. We attend courses and workshops, or read books about methods and techniques, and then just find ourselves eventually trying some of that out in our work with students. This is ultimately an inefficient method of professional development, however, because it depends on whim or chance for its application. Unfortunately, many brilliant teaching ideas never get tried out. Some ideas which are tried and proven successful never get instituted on a regular basis because they are forgotten or only used when we happen to think about them during planning sessions. Most of the good educational curricula that might be of value to a special educator are never tried and used because there is just too much of it and no way of regularly taking a look at what we know to see what could be useful in specific teaching situations. The needs, moods, styles, philosophies and opinions, as well as the specific job placements of teachers, change with time. Things that weren't important at one time in your career or at one stage during the year become relevant later on. Materials which did not seem appropriate to the needs of one child can become essential to the needs of another child. Unless we plan to write books, curriculum guides, articles, or programs, it seems that we often don't look at how to put together all that we have learned, to enable us to teach more effectively. All teachers should have some kind of resource system which enables them to efficiently retrieve teaching skills, strategies, interventions, techniques, approaches, materials, and methods so that they are able to put them directly into practice when the need arises. This is particularly necessary for the special educator who must meet the needs of individual children with varied ability levels, learning styles and modes, interests and strengths.

Writing teaching approaches into your program provides such a system for efficient retrieval of relevant materials and methods. After having completed this final stage of your instructional program sheet (the teaching approaches column) you will be able to locate the skills which are important to a given child's needs and find teaching tools written there, which:

1. Are directly available to you;
2. Encompass a variety of uses and needs;
3. Are tools that you have used in the past, enjoyed using, and know are effective.

It will be a system which you can continually add to as you encounter further materials and methods in your professional development.

As a first step in developing this aspect of the program, you can go through the instructional program sheets for which you have developed specific skills and write in under teaching approaches the methods and materials which you know are available to you in some form and which are directly applicable to each given skill. If you wish to be more systematic, however, use the inventory of present teaching resources worksheet on the following page. By completing this inventory, you will know at a glance what your present resources are in each area (hardware, software, professional materials, and methods). This can prepare you more completely for the task of filling in teaching approaches on the final form. By filling in the inventory worksheet, you will become aware of which teaching areas lack materials or methods; and this can provide valuable information to you on areas of need, and tell you the kinds of materials or training you need to get for yourself.

Definition of Terms Used in the Inventory of Present Teaching Resources Worksheet

Hardware:
  concrete materials
  manipulatives
  art materials
  building supplies
  tools
  media equipment
  other non-print educational materials
Software:
  textbooks
  books
  workbooks
  dittos
  records
  tapes
  slides, etc.
Professional Materials:
  magazine articles
  photocopied handouts
  pamphlets
  professional books
  other materials which you have acquired in your
    training and professional development which have
    been helpful to you in particular areas.
Preferred Techniques, Strategies, and Interventions:
  Here can be listed those kinds of teaching methods

FIGURE 3.1. *Inventory of Present Teaching Resources.*

Area	Hardware	Software	Professional Mat's	Strategies, etc.
Math Computation	abacus, calculator, poker chips, beans, board games	math ditto sheets, Spectrum math workbooks (10), state series math textbooks (8)	xeroxed article by Bob Wirtz on rote skills, article by Craig Pearson in *Learning* on chisanbop	math games, use of rhythm and music to learn basic facts, chip trading for regrouping skills, use of real-life problems
Auditory Memory	musical instruments, cassette recorder and tapes, record player and records	book of poems and songs to memorize, Lindamood program	*Activities for Developing Auditory Perception* by P. Behrmann (Academic Therapy Pub's.)	memorize poems and songs of high-interest; story-telling; kids retell story; memorize each other's phone no's.
Vocational Skills (typing)	3 typewriters, 2 typing stands,	typing texts, corrasible bond (2	none	balance the procedures of

	1 metronome, white-out fluid	reams), ditto masters of practice lessons		touch typing patterns with chance to "hunt and peck" name, spelling lists, etc.
Self-Concept	puppets and theater-art materials, mirrors, drama costumes	teacher-made personal attitude questionnaires	*101 Ways to Enhance Self-Concept in the Classroom* by Jack Canfield (Prentice Hall)	students need to make and do things they feel good about; values clarification activities
Geography	globe, map of the world, puzzles of the states, protractors and compasses (10)	state series textbooks on geography (grades 3-5, 5 each), ditto masters (different levels), dittoed maps of U.S. and the world	none	relate geography to child's personal sense of space, inner maps; start by mapping body, then room, then school, neighborhood, city, state, country; use images to assoc. places.

which you find particularly helpful in teaching or dealing with a particular area, skill, or situation.

Once you have finished filling out the inventory worksheet, take the resources listed and plug them in under teaching approaches on the instructional program sheets you have developed for your program. You may use the same teaching resource or method for more than one skill area or specific skill. You may wish to put in as many possible teaching techniques and strategies as you have available, particularly if you only have a few at first. Or, you may wish to restrict yourself only to those techniques which have worked for you, which you feel good about, or which have worked for colleagues and other programs you know about. There is no point in listing materials and methods you will never use. Yet, it is often difficult to say exactly when a given tool may prove useful in the future under circumstances you may not at present clearly envision. Another advantage of keeping an inventory worksheet is that you can put down only relevant teaching tools onto the instructional program sheets and still be able to refer back to your total body of available resources on the inventory worksheet. These materials and methods may become relevant to your needs later on, and can then be placed on the program sheets.

List a variety of tools and approaches for each skill which can meet different needs you may encounter in the children you work with. Just as you needed to consider several factors in your selection of assessment tools, so too you need to keep in mind the following factors in your choice of which teaching tools to employ for a specific skill in a given situation:

1. *Learning channel*—You should have a sense of the perceptual roadways that each tool employs. You can even write, in parentheses, at the end of each tool, which particular learning channels are engaged (visual-motor, auditory-oral, etc.).

2. *Learning style*—You should be sensitive to the more general social, emotional, and temperamental learning factors which govern the appropriateness of each teaching tool. These include such factors as materials to engage a highly active imagination, materials which will not overly stimulate a restless child, materials which can greatly challenge

an unmotivated child, or which will not overly challenge an easily frustrated child.

3. *Specific interests and strengths*—Look at the materials and methods which might specifically engage the interests of a particular child. For example, providing a spaceship model building kit for a child with fine-motor skill needs who has a mania for extra-terrestrial activities.

4. *Classroom organization*—Note those materials and methods which can be used only individually, those which can be used in small group situations, those which take a long time to use or require several sessions, those which require a lot of pre-class teacher preparation, and those which are ready to use as is.

5. *Teacher attitude*—It is also important to look at your own personal attitude toward the materials and methods suggested. The extent to which you are excited and enthusiastic about a given material or method can be a big factor toward generating learning in that area. It may be useful for you, in fact, to explore why a particular material is not stimulating or useful to you. Materials which are dissatisfying to you or which you feel are not effective tools should be left out of your program. It is not worth running the risk of turning off children to a skill because your own attitude toward the materials and methods you are using is negative. You might find it helpful to list those factors which are important to you in educating students and use that as a guide in selecting materials for your program. Here is my own personal list:

*Factors That Are Important for Me
in Educating Students*

—Feelings
—Use of the body
—Use of imagination
—Creativity
—Child's personal world
—Immediate feedback to the child
—Giving the child choices
—Self-esteem

FIGURE 3.2. Instructional Program Sheet with All Columns Completed.

Skills	Assessments	Criteria	Goals	Approaches
Able to compute basic addition facts — on sums to 10 — on sums to 18	1. chalkboard exam; note strategy used 2. teacher-made ditto 3. oral quiz 4. peer given flashcards	100% 9 out of 10 problems given	Given a teacher-made ditto of 10 addition problems with sums of . . ., the student will correctly solve . . . of the problems.	Rhythm games, chanting or singing facts, chisanbop, cuisenaire rods, adding real things, magic squares, nomogram, flashcards
Able to compute addition problems of — 2 digits plus 2 digits with no regrouping	1. teacher-made skill card 2. dittoed worksheet page	70 - 90% depending on student	Given a dittoed worksheet page of 10 problems involving . . . digit plus . . . digit addition without regroup, the student will solve . . . of them.	Use lattice format; graph paper; work with directionality, right to left; mnemonic techniques related to body.
— 3 digits plus 3 digits with no regrouping	1. teacher-made skill card 2. dittoed work-	same as above		

-54-

Objective	Materials	Criterion	Conditions	Activities
— 2 digits plus 2 digits with re-grouping — 3 digits plus 3 digits with 2 regroupings	sheet page 1. teacher-made skill card 2. dittoed work-sheet page 3. abacus; note strategy when re-grouping	same as above same as above	Given a teacher-made skill card of 10 problems involving . . . digit plus . . . digit addition with (1,2) regroupings, the student will solve . . . of them.	Use place value activities for re-grouping; chip trading, abacus, Dienes blocks; use images for concept of carrying (elf has too many bricks, gives to big brother who makes into one big brick, etc.)
Able to add columns of — 3 one-digit numbers — columns of 5 two-digit numbers	1. chalkboard exam; note strategy used 2. teacher-made ditto 3. beans as counters: note how uses	80% 70%	Given 10 problems on the chalkboard involving column addition of (3,5) (1,2) digit numbers, the student will solve . . . of them.	Add lists of real things (money, candy, time, etc.)

- —Peer relationships
- —Concrete practical materials
- —Real-life situations
- —Playing games and having fun while learning
- —Music and rhythm

When you have written your present teaching resources into their appropriate places under the teaching approaches column of each instructional program sheet you have developed, note which specific skills do not contain any teaching approaches or are limited to only one method or material. These can be areas of priority for you as you determine the kinds of materials you need to acquire in the future or the kind of specific training you would like to obtain from inservice workshops or other sources of professional improvement. It may be unnecessary to acquire specific teaching resources for a given skill until a practical situation emerges (such as having to teach a child or group of children that particular skill) which will require your spending some time in planning sessions, researching appropriate techniques or locating relevant materials. In any case, having written teaching approaches into your program will save you time in future planning sessions and will enable you to quickly locate and implement the means by which to teach the skills that become part of the IEPs of the children you work with. Some IEP forms contain a section after the instructional goals which asks you to list methods and materials used to achieve the stated objective. You will be able to transfer information from your instructional program sheet directly to the IEP form and save yourself from having to rethink and redevelop materials and methods for each new IEP which you complete. At the same time, the challenges you face with each new child and IEP can provide the basis for continuing the process of building onto your program.

Organizing Your Teaching Resources so that They Can Be Readily Found, Used, and Added Onto

Here are some suggestions for ways to organize the materials and methods which have been listed in your program so that they can be easily located, used to teach specific skills, and added onto as you discover new methods and materials in the course of your professional development. You will be more likely to use a method or material which can be referred to quickly than one which requires going down to the library to research or hunting for a misplaced magazine article or searching your classroom closets for a teaching aid you used at the beginning of the year but had forgotten about.

Shoe box labs. Hardware materials for specific skills can be stored in shoe boxes, hat boxes, or other containers. Here are some examples of materials which might be found in a typical shoe box lab, taken from each of the five basic skill categories which make up the "universe of skills."

Category: Basic Academic Skills
Area: math/number theory
Skill: place value
Contents of container:
    chip trading game
    small abacus
    mechanical calculator
    groups of popsicle sticks with beans glued on
    multi-base converter

Category: Human Processing Skills
Area: visual perception
Contents of container:
    optical illusions
    Polaroid camera
    simple animation devices
    kaleidoscope
    magnifying glass
    pieces of colored cellophane
    geometric designs

Category: Practical Life Skills
Area: personal finances
Contents of container:
    practice checkbooks
    copy of Sylvia Porter's *Money Book*
    a budget ledger
    applications for bank and credit accounts
    pocket calculator

Category: Behavioral/Affective/Social Skills
Area: self-concept

Contents of container:
    puppets
    appropriate story books
    record of self-concept songs
    mirrors
    "warm fuzzies"

Category: Content/Knowledge Skills
Area: French language
Contents of container:
    dictionary
    flashcards
    board game
    French comic book

Of course, you might need to use certain materials for several different skill areas and not be able to keep them in any one box. This could be solved by keeping commonly used materials in a certain area of the classroom and indicating on a card kept in each box where the commonly used materials for that particular skill or skill group can be found. Shoe box labs can be used by the teacher solely for retrieval purposes; or, they can be organized to enable the students to use them independently. A cassette tape or a printed card of instructions can then be included to provide directions to the students in using the materials contained in the box. You may wish to keep all your cassette tapes in one central place as an "activity tape library."

Skill centers. Another way of organizing materials according to skills involves the technique of creating learning centers around specific skills or skill areas which represent common needs for several children in the program. Materials could be arranged in such a way that children would be able to use them with minimal teacher assistance. Activity cards could be written to direct the children in their learning. Here are some examples of activities which could be included for areas from each of our five basic skill categories:

Category: Basic Academic Skills
Area: writing/handwriting
Activities:
    play a game identifying each other's handwriting
    practice handwriting using a variety of tools and pa-
        per (pens, pencils, crayons, ink quills, various sizes,

colors, and shapes of paper)

have on display different models of beautiful handwriting to trace or copy

create art projects from activity cards which require
repetitive handwriting of different kinds

have available materials for developing fine motor
development (templates, stencils, mazes, tremor
control device etc.)

Category: Human Processing Skills
Area: auditory perception
Activities:

record and play back voices

play auditory sequencing games

use different kinds of materials for developing auditory sensitivity (stethoscope, tuning fork, tin can
walkie-talkie, earplugs, etc.)

listen to auditory materials of different kinds (records, tapes etc.)

Category: Practical Life Skills
Area: nutrition
Activities:

complete questionnaires on personal eating habits

compare and contrast the food values of different
canned goods using information on their labels

do problems based on charts containing information
about food groups, food additives etc.

do math problems based on weights and measurements of canned goods

Category: Behavioral/Affective/Social Skills
Area: positive social interaction
Activities:

students write "warm fuzzies" to each other

students record into a tape recorder nice things
about themselves and play it back

read the book *I Am Loveable and Capable* by Sid
Simon

listen to a tape recording of self-concept story

Category: Content/Knowledge Skills
Area: geography/specific academic textbook
Activities:

have materials available for two or three projects

which the text suggests

have library books and other reading materials which were recommended as Further Reading at the end of given chapters

take a concept in the book which seemed especially vague or abstract and illustrate it through pictures, materials, or other concrete means

have students rewrite portions of the textbook in their own language and keep the student-written book in the skill center for others to read

Whether or not you use these particular suggestions, it is a good idea to keep materials which will be used for common skill groups in the same area such as a closet, a shelf, or a section of the room.

Worksheet file. This is an idea for teachers who do not like to use workbooks because their students do not need much of what is in the workbook or may be confused visually by the layout. There may be certain pages which deal with a particular skill which the teacher would like to use, however. Simply tear out pages from consumable workbooks, or even sections of pages to make the visual input less intense, and mount on cardboard or construction paper. You can laminate the workbook pages and have students do the pages with a grease pencil or projection pen. These pages can be filed according to specific skill and can transform a collection of consumable worksheets into a functional system that will plug right into your program. You can also file relevant ditto masters by skill and run off copies according to your needs. A number of reproducible books are also available, as well as computer software.

Idea file. This is a way of "grounding" ideas which you encounter in books, magazines, and other written sources. You can file them according to the skills with which they deal. Magazine articles from professional teaching journals can be photocopied or torn out. Handouts from inservice workshops, pieces of paper with your own ideas written on them, designs for games, curriculum materials, and miscellaneous ideas can all be filed according to specific skills or skill area. Written materials that are used a lot in your work can be laminated or mounted on construction paper for sturdier use.

Recipe box file. Ideas, methods, or other resources which you may overhear in a teacher's lounge, at a workshop or which may simply occur to you at some point in or out of school, can be jotted down on 3x5 or 4x6 index cards and filed according to skill. This file can then be referred to when you are sitting down in front of your plan book. Some of the kinds of ideas you can include in your file are:

1. Step-by-step sequencing of an idea or method
2. Materials for a project
3. Where to go for further information on an idea
4. Factors to consider in implementing an activity
5. Related activities to consider
6. Initial ideas which can be developed later
7. Passages from books or quotations which give depth to an idea or justify it academically

Game file. If you use board games extensively in teaching specific skills, they can be made from standard Manila file folders or other convenient uniform materials and filed according to specific skill.

Textbook correlations. Several formal assessment tools and instructional programs offer correlations of certain skill-based components of their own program with several leading textbooks in given areas. Unless you have the time and are interested in this sort of thing, you would probably be best off obtaining samples of these textbook correlations if you plan to use textbooks in your teaching, rather than developing your own correlations. These correlations can then be put directly to work in terms of your own program by writing them in under teaching approaches on the instructional program sheets. Specific sections of textbooks can then be used to teach specific skills.

Personal professional library. Your own collection of professional books, pamphlets, flyers, brochures, and other materials should be kept available and accessible to you when you do your planning. Of particular value are those publications which deal with practical activities in specific skill areas which are relevant to your job. These can be stored by skill area in special library storage units designed to contain printed matter. It can also increase the likelihood that those ideas to which you have been exposed as an educator will find their way quickly and effectively into practice in your program.

Chapter 4

Where You Are Going to Keep Track of Who Has Learned What
A Simple, Clear, and Effective Means of Recordkeeping

You have finished compiling the instructional program sheets and are ready to put the program to work. You are working with children, assessing them, establishing areas of need, and perhaps writing IEPs. You need, at this point, a recordkeeping system which will enable you to keep track of assessment results, plan activities around common needs, pinpoint specific instructional goals for each child, and keep track of each child's progress with respect to the specific instructional goals written. Before you begin this process of actually working with students, you need to transfer the skills you will be working with—all or part of the total bank of skills from your program—onto a group progress form, horizontally, and list the names of the students in your program vertically. A sample of the group progress form has been included on the next page. List on each group progress form the skill area or sub-area (as for example, math/computation, addition and subtraction). Then, as you begin to assess each child, you can keep track of your results directly on the group progress chart, utilizing the following symbol-key as an aid to recognizing at a glance each child's relationship to any given skill. This symbol-key will provide, in addition, an easy way of determining group needs for planning small-group activities during the year.

FIGURE 4.1. *Group Progress Chart.*

MATH Computation addition and subtraction	+facts to 10	+facts to 18	22 +31	323 +114	27 +39	348 +239	388 +267	4267 +1867
Joe	●	●	●	●	●	◐		
Ed	●	●	●	●	◐	○		
Randy	●	●	●	●	●	●	●	●
Sam	●	◐	◐					
David	●	●	●	●	●	◐	○	
Peter	●	●	●	●	●	●	●	◐
Mary	●	●	●	●	●	●	●	◐
Betsy	●	●	●	◐	○	○		
Kristy	●	●	●	●	●	●	●	
Susan	●	●	●	●	●	◐	○	

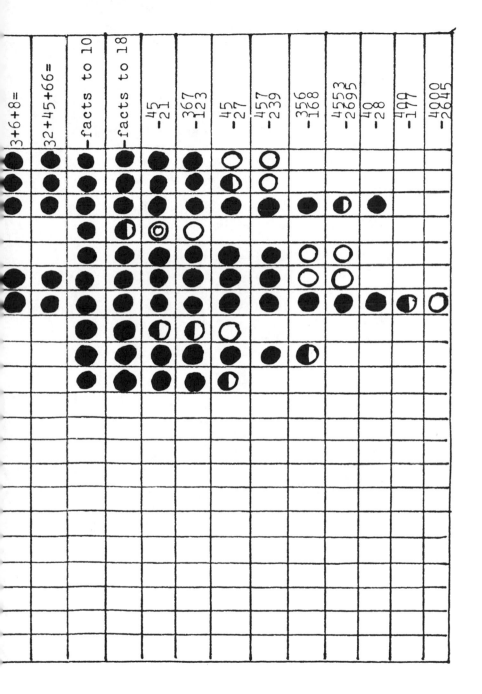

Symbol-Key for Group Progress Chart

Empty space:
> child has not yet been assessed.

Circle completely filled in with blue:
> student has achieved mastery level on skill during first assessment; date of assessment can be written in.

Circle partially filled in with blue:
> Student was assessed in skill and shows some ability but has not yet achieved mastery; the extent to which the circle is filled in can parallel the degree to which the student has approached mastery.

Unfilled circle:
> student was assessed in skill and shows little or no proficiency.

Circle completely filled in with red:
> student was initially assessed and showed no proficiency, was assessed at some point during the program and achieved mastery level; date of mastery can be written in.

Circle partially filled in with red:
> student was initially assessed and didn't know the skill; was assessed during the program and achieved partial mastery.

Circle partially filled in with blue, partially with red:
> student was initially assessed and found to have partial proficiency in skill, was assessed later during the program and achieved mastery.

Circle with smaller concentric circles inside:
> student was assessed on more than one occasion with still no acquired proficiency in the skill; number of circles can correspond to number of assessments.

Slash:
> given skill not relevant to student's needs.

Such a key provides a quick shorthand way to determine skill acquisition patterns both with the individual and among groups of students. The color-coded patterns which emerge on the group chart can allow you to graphically see areas of existing competence (solid blue), areas of need (empty or partially filled circles), and areas of progress and achievement (partial or solid red circles).

The group progress chart can be used at different stages of the IEP process:

1. Before the IEP has been written, to get information on specific areas of need to be included in the team evaluation of the child's progress needs;
2. During the development of the IEP, to help determine general goals to be written into the plan;
3. During the development of specific instructional goals within the IEP, to help pinpoint specific skill needs;
4. During the implementation of the IEP, to assess progress in those areas and skills written into the IEP and to indicate when specific goals have been met;
5. During the implementation of the IEP, to continue the assessment process in areas not specifically written into the IEP but which may provide additional data requiring a modification in the original IEP.

This information can be helpful in a variety of ways to the different parties involved in the IEP process:

1. Communicating quick assessment information to the evaluation team responsible for developing the goals of the IEP;
2. Communicating to parents a child's current levels of skill acquisition and progress in the program;
3. Communicating information to the child about his functioning level, things at which he or she excels, or needs further work on;
4. Communicating quick skill-related information to regular classroom teachers and other specialists responsible for the child's education, to enable them to correlate their own programs accordingly and provide for each child's level of skill attainment;
5. Serving as a means of self-communication for you in the course of curricular planning for individuals and

groups of students in the program. Skills in which several individuals show needs can be focused on in terms of group learning where appropriate, whereas isolated skill needs can be focused on in a 1-to-1 setting. Peer teaching can be utilized since information is easily accessible concerning students who know a skill and can teach it to those who do not know the skill. Attainment goals as indicated in red on the sheet serve as tangible visible feedback to the teacher on the effectiveness of the methods and materials being used in the program.

The group progress chart provides quick summary information related to skill acquisition among individuals and groups. It does not provide specific information related to those skills, in terms of performance levels, conditions under which each skill was learned, or other relevant data. For this purpose, an individual progress chart is provided. The individual progress chart can include data which is initially gathered in the process of creating an IEP or assessing basic program needs for an individual; but its main purpose is to keep track of individual educational goals which have been created for a student. Several kinds of data can be included on the individual progress chart:

1. Assessment data, which can indicate how close the student is to meeting the criterion established in the instructional goal included in the IEP.
2. Information concerning obstacles to achieving the goal; things the student does not yet understand; subskills the student does not yet possess; emotional or social factors which may be getting in the way of the student learning the skill; unproductive learning strategies; misunderstandings or confusions. Data from this category can lead to the creation of new goals which must be mastered before current goals can be met.
3. Information concerning positive means of teaching a particular skill to a particular student; notes on what materials or other factors accompanied a particularly good learning session.
4. Final evaluation data; once a goal has been achieved, all the information which went into assessing the

skill at a level of mastery can be stated, including test scores, performance data, and anecdotal information. A symbol such as a smiling face can be used in the final box of the goal on the chart to indicate that this particular goal has been achieved.

The process of selecting which goals are to be focused upon for inclusion in the individual progress chart can be based on any of several factors. General goals written by the evaluation team can serve as a guideline for the more specific goals to be included. Among all the skills a student may need to work on, certain of these skills may have a higher priority than others and need to be included first in the individual progress chart. Certain skills must be mastered before other related skills of need can be undertaken. Some skills tie in more closely to a child's survival needs in a particular learning environment and should be focused upon first. In addition, you don't want to write up more goals than you feel you can conceivably achieve over a given period of time. You might want to write up a certain group of short-term goals for a given period of time and leave other areas of need for later, when these initial, higher-priority goals have been met. Writing up too few goals may not accurately reflect the child's educational needs. Writing up too many short-term goals may make educational planning too confusing or overwhelming. Restricting yourself to well chosen, relevant, high-priority goals that are tied in with the broader goals written by the educational assessment team allows you to focus on what is most immediately relevant to the child's educational needs. As these are completed, new short-term goals can always be written in.

Choose the specific goals you would like to focus on with each child by referring to the group progress chart. Outline in pencil or pen the squares on the group progress chart which represent those skill areas of need which you would like to encompass within short-term goals on the individual progress chart. Once each goal has been determined and blocked out on the group progress chart, you can proceed to transfer that skill onto the individual progress charts. An example of a completed individual progress chart has been included on the following page. Individual progress charts should be kept for each child. Several sheets may be required for each child, depending upon the number of goals written and the time period involved in working with the child. List the specific goals

FIGURE 4.2. Individual Progress Chart.

Addition of two digit plus two digit numbers with regrouping 80% mastery	9-15 0%; puts down tens value in answer instead of regrouping 26 +39 515	9-20 started working w/ chip trading game to work on place value; enjoys-likes to stack chips by color/value
Will learn to type and show proficiency by identifying from touch 15/26 letter keys	9-13 Introduced to basic parts of typewriter; very excited;getting one for Xmas if he does well.	9-15 keys are capped;this upsets him at first but he did a line of fj,fj,fj etc.
Will show enhanced self-concept by decrease in neg self-statements 10/wk to 0/wk	9-8 I observed following statements: art: "This ain't no good";Math:"I'm lousy in it."	10-5 Drew 3 pictures of things he does well; week of 10-5 8 neg.self-statements
Will identify names of 45/50 states of U.S. point to outline map of U.S. in naming	9-12 knows 10/50; knows 8 states more by name but incorrectly placed;	9-20 working daily w/ puzzle of U.S. names states for aide as he puts pieces together
Will remember seven digit phone numbers (8 out of 10) Auditory Memory Skill	9-7 remembered 10/10 phone numbers;on original assess. was he motivated? Check.	9-9 Original tester reports negative behavior in test; Unhappy about missing P.E.

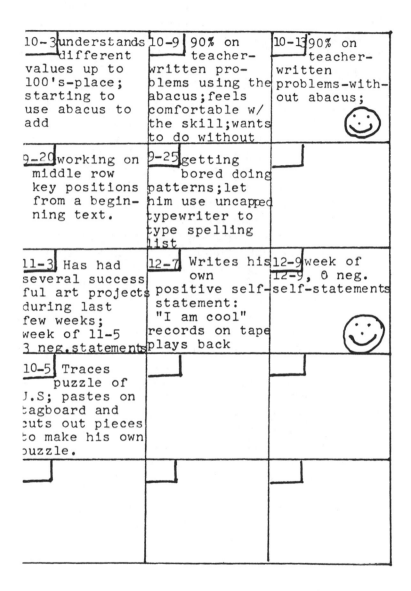

10-3 understands different values up to 100's-place; starting to use abacus to add	10-9 90% on teacher-written pro-blems using the abacus;feels comfortable w/ the skill;wants to do without	10-13 90% on teacher-written problems-with-out abacus; ☺
9-20 working on middle row key positions from a begin-ning text.	9-25 getting bored doing patterns;let him use uncapped typewriter to type spelling list	
11-3 Has had several success-ful art projects during last few weeks; week of 11-5 3 neg.statements	12-7 Writes his own positive self-statement: "I am cool" records on tape plays back	12-9 week of 12-9, 0 neg. self-statements ☺
10-5 Traces puzzle of J.S; pastes on tagboard and cuts out pieces to make his own puzzle.		

for each child on the spaces provided on the individual progress chart. Once you begin working with each child on specific skills, this individualized recordkeeping device will enable you to keep track of the child's progress with respect to each specific goal. The small boxes in the upper left-hand corner of each square are for dating each piece of information. This individual progress chart can be useful in several ways:

1. In the initial stages of assessment, all relevant information can be included on these pages. Since the group progress chart indicates only whether a skill has been mastered or not, the individual progress chart can be used to record more specific information related to each assessment. This can then form the starting point for deciding which skills you intend to focus upon later.

2. As a means of reporting to parents, teachers, administrators, and students, progress in specific goals, giving detailed information about where the student is along the pathway to mastery, what particular things are standing in the way of further progress, and what things have been helpful in moving toward the goal. This information can be relayed to support personnel working with the child and be used to reinforce their work with the student.

3. As a means of planning future curricular strategies in each skill, avoiding strategies which are not productive with a particular child, and developing methods and materials which seem to bear fruit; helping to pin down the exact source of the difficulties in terms of subskills needed, strategies, and misconceptions, to deal with any social or emotional factors which need to be addressed.

4. As a means of efficiently transferring evaluation information directly to the evaluation section of an IEP form. Instead of having to turn to several different sources of information to put together the results of an evaluation on a specific skill, you have already kept it all together and simply need to refer to the individual progress chart and transfer that information onto the IEP form. Usually, you can simply include the data from the square farthest to the right for each skill, indicating the farthest extent

toward mastery which the student has attained (or mastery itself). You can also include any relevant information from this chart which will provide a clear and complete account of the evaluation for the IEP records.

Student Progress Chart

The student progress chart is a means by which you can provide the student with simple, clear, visual feedback about his progress with respect to specific educational goals. You may wish to record only certain goals from the individual progress chart onto the student progress chart. Some goals are more easily objectified on the bar graph included on the student progress chart. In addition, you will want to only include goals here which the student can clearly understand and relate to his or her sense of educational achievement.

Once the goals have been listed on the student progress chart, a teacher-student conference is recommended, when practical, to go over the goals and make sure that the student understands what is involved with each goal. The student can be told that his or her time in the program will be spent at least in part in working on these goals, and that mastery of the goals represents an important part of his or her educational progress in school. Depending upon the ability and interest of the student, he or she can be given responsibility for keeping the student progress chart and filling in new evaluation data for each goal when it becomes available. If the chart is kept in a readily available location, such as the student's desk or personal folder, it can serve as a constant reminder to the student of his or her progress in the program and hopefully act as a positive stimulus for further achievement in these and succeeding objectives.

FIGURE 4.3. Student Progress Chart.

	0%	10%	20%	30%
two digits + two digits w/regrouping				
two digits – two digits w/regrouping				
read 3rd grade passage with 95% accuracy				
Remember seven digit numbers				
Spell 3rd grade list w/ 80% accuracy				
Form 26/26 lower case cursive letters				
Identify 15/26 letters on typewriter by touch				
Decrease neg. self-state-ments to 0/wk				
Identify 45/50 states of U.S.				

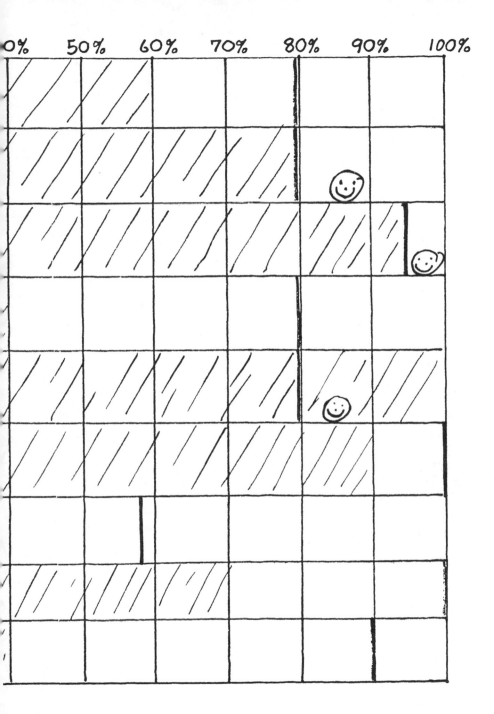

Chapter 5

When You Have Put It All Together

This book should be seen as a flexible tool to be used by you, the special educator, in ways that seem most appropriate to your individual needs. By no means is it expected that you should use all of the elements contained in this book to structure all of the skill areas and learning needs you will be responsible for in your educational work. This would be a monumental undertaking. Rather, it is expected that you will use those parts of this book which seem relevant, to structure certain areas of your educational work in ways that can be useful to you. This book provides an organizational matrix which can be applied in widely varied circumstances to make sense of what might otherwise be a chaotic profusion of data. It may seem to require a large investment of time to apply. This investment will easily pay off, however, once the structures have been created and the process of using them has begun. Among the benefits which can emerge from having applied some or all of the organizational suggestions of this book:

1. You can use your program from year to year even when your job situation changes; simply readjust the skills to become relevant to your current job placement. As you progress in your career, your

bank of skills, assessment tools, goals, and teaching approaches become more varied and rich as a permanent professional resource.

2. While putting the program together, you have learned a great deal about the processes involved in skill building, resource and curriculum development, and educational evaluation. You can use the information which you have learned to help other people. You can share your information on curriculum committees, parent-teacher committees, with other teachers in the context of inservice workshops or in support groups. In addition, since you have developed many valuable teaching skills while developing your own program, you can add this information to your resume in searching for other jobs in education, or can even apply the skills you learned in fields other than education (business, merchandising, psychology, etc.).

3. If you have put together a program which you feel represents a very positive addition to the field of education, you can publish it, do workshops on it, send it to ERIC for inclusion in their computerized reference system, or make copies of it and offer it to your district, to other teachers, or other educational personnel for use in their programs.

Ultimately, this guide points toward a lifelong process of learning, developing and acquiring skills, and putting them to work in the universal classroom of life. I hope that the structures which have been presented in this book will be a positive contribution to your professional growth.

Afterword
Beyond Classroom Structure

The word *structure* is golden in education. How often have you heard a teacher criticized for not providing students with enough structure? How many children have been referred to your program with a note in their accumulated file saying "needs a structured environment"? The word gets used so often, in so many ways, that we take its own structure for granted, not realizing that there are many different structures that make up a classroom (as you should by now realize after wending your way through this small book!).

Educational researchers have worked for decades and spent billions of dollars in an attempt to determine what kinds of structures work best in promoting effective learning. This book has not duplicated their efforts. What it has done is to provide a meta-structure, or a methodology by which teachers can determine their own structures and utilize those structures which work best for them. With so many static structures out on the market (diagnostic-prescriptive learning systems, curriculum kits, behavior modification programs, and so on), I have attempted to provide a structure that breathes, one that you, the teacher, can adapt to your own needs, just as you adapt your environment to the needs of your students.

Of course, there are rigidities even in what I have provided here. No structure is entirely free of them. The progress charts, inventories, and program sheets in this book may seem like just more of the same old teacher's stuff to you. If these forms do not "feel right" to you, I would urge you to modify them, even abandon them, and create forms that work for you (perhaps forms you've been using all along with great success) or work without any charts or graphs at all. Teachers have the same kind of tremendous range in teaching styles that students have in learning styles: divergent/convergent, intuitive/intellectual, linear/holistic, etc. The important thing is that you work within your own style of teaching. Perhaps this book has been of some help to you in clarifying certain things about your own teaching style and preferences. Knowing this can help you make even greater use of the material in this book by picking and choosing those elements that appeal to you and rejecting what is foreign. The final product will probably (perhaps even hopefully) not even resemble what lies between the covers of this book, but instead will be an organic structure that will live and breathe as you go about the important task of helping children learn.

This leads me to my final point. Something lies beyond classroom structure: you and the children with whom you work. A teacher can have the most efficient super-duper electronic whiz-bang curriculum on earth, yet without the living-breathing relationship of teacher and student, all that paraphernalia and all those techniques and methods and systems and charts and graphs count for nought. One of the great failings of education (special or otherwise) has been its own failure to recognize this fact. Thirty years ago, Arthur Jersild wrote a book entitiled *When Teachers Face Themselves.* This remarkable work agued that until teachers look within themselves and learn to deal with their own inner lives (their joys, sorrows, angers, anxieties, etc.), their task of teaching will be very difficult. Even further back, in the 1920s, a German educator, Rudolf Steiner, was saying very much the same thing: "What kind of school plan you make is neither here nor there; what matters is what sort of a person you are" (*The Kingdom of Childhood,* p. 32).

This is at once the most simple and the most complex thing to understand. It is based on the premise that children are exceedingly sensitive to the inner lives of adults; much more sensitive than is commonly acknowledged by teachers or parents. This is probably even more true with children who have been referred to special education programs. This profound truth—"know thyself"—is based on the premise that much more goes on between student and teacher than meets the eye. The field of education has been trying for many years now to pin down exactly what it is that occurs in the interaction between student and teacher that spells the difference between success and failure in learning. Yet it is unlikely that videotapes or observational checklists will ever reveal the vast interaction of feeling, mood, manner, and style which goes on beneath the surface of the school day. This used to be called the "hidden curriculum." While this phrase has gone the way of all educational fads, its truth lives on in the inner lives of teachers and students going about their work in the classroom. It is found in a teacher's comments at the end of the day: "Oh what a *day* I had!", "That kid drove me up the wall!", "The most *beautiful* thing happened in class today!" It is also found in the unsaid fears, angers, hurts, joys, prides, and thrills of a child walking home from school. These human events cannot be plotted on any graph or charted on any IEP form, yet they comprise the single most important factor in the learning process.

The point, then, that I would like to leave with you is this: while classroom structures undoubtedly help to mold the conditions through which these human events occur, they cannot take the place of a living classroom relationship between you and your students. You probably are wondering why I have chosen to leave this sage bit until the end or even to include it at all in a book about practical classroom structures. Perhaps it is because one must first create the classroom strucures within which all of this human interaction can take place. Then one has the freedom beyond classroom structure to enjoy each new moment with students without worrying about where things are and what needs to be done. A person who runs a chaotic classroom—I can testify from personal experience—has little time left for knowing either oneself or one's students. I hope that this book can offer you some small liberation from the Scylla of classroom chaos and the Charybdis of rigid commercial kits and programs. I wish you good luck in your efforts to create a living classroom structure!

Appendix
Selected Resources

General: Special Needs

Grahl, Ursula. 1970. *The Exceptional Child.* Letchworth, Hertfordshire: Rudolf Steiner Press.

Hawkins, F. 1975. *The logic of action.* New York: Pantheon.

Holt, J. 1964. *How children fail.* New York: Dell.

Kraus, R. 1971. *Leo the latebloomer.* New York: Young Readers Press.

Lederman, J. 1979. *Anger and the rocking chair.* New York: McGraw-Hill.

Meisels, S. J., ed. 1979. *Special education and development: perspectives on young children with special needs.* Baltimore: University Park Press.

Schrag, P., and Divoky, D. 1979. *The myth of the hyperactive child.* New York: Dell.

von Hilshiemer, G. 1973. *How to live with your special child.* Washington, D. C.: Acropolis.

Formal Assessment

Coles, G. S. 1978. The learning disability test battery: empirical and social issues. *Harvard Educational Review* 48: 313-340.

Johnson, O. G. 1976. *Tests and measurements in child development: handbooks I and II.* San Francisco: Jossey-Bass.

Mauser, A. J. 1981. *Assessing the learning disabled: selected instruments,* 3rd ed. Novato, California: Academic Therapy.

Informal Assessment

Almy, M., and Genishi, C. 1979. *Ways of studying children.* New York: Teachers College Press.

Carini, P. 1973. The Prospect School, taking account of progress. *Childhood Education* 49:350-356.

Langstaff, N. 1975. *Teaching in an open classroom: informal checks, diagnoses and learning strategies for beginning reading and math.* Boston: National Association of Independent Schools.

Richardson, E. 1964. *In the early world.* New York: Pantheon.

Writing Instructional Goals

Arena, J. 1978. *How to write an IEP.* Novato, California: Academic Therapy.

Mager, R. F. 1975. *Preparing instructional objectives.* Belmont, California: Fearon.

Organizing Instructional Resources

Engel, B. 1973. *Arranging the informal classroom.* Newton, Massachusetts: Educational Development Center.

Gingell, L. P. 1973. *The ABC's of the open classroom.* Homewood, Illinois: ETC Pubs.

Kaplan, S. N., et al. 1973. *Change for children: ideas and activities for individualizing learning.* Pacific Palisades, California: Goodyear.

Thomas, J. I. 1975. *Learning centers.* Boston: Holbrook.

Teaching Approaches in the Five Skill Areas

Reading:

Ashton-Warner, Sylvia. 1964. *Teacher.* New York: Bantam.
Bettelheim, Bruno and Zelan, Karen. 1982. *On learning to read: the child's fascination with meaning.* New York: Knopf.
Kohl, Herbert. 1973. *Reading, how to.* New York: E. P. Dutton.
Moffet, James. 1973. *A student-centered language arts curriculum: grades K-6.* Boston: Houghton-Mifflin.
Trelease, Jim. 1982. *The read aloud handbook.* Harmondsworth, England: Penguin.

Writing:

Brown, Rosellen, et al. 1972. *The whole word catelogue.* New York: Virgil Books.
Kock, Kenneth. 1971. *Wishes, lies and dreams: teaching children to write poetry.* New York: Vintage.
Zavatsky, Bill and Padgett, Ron. 1977. *The whole word catelogue 2.* New York: McGraw-Hill.

Spelling:

Barsch, Ray H. 1974. *a, e, i, o, u . . . and sometimes y: 109 fun ways to enjoy and improve spelling in the classroom.* Canoga Park, California: Ray Barsch Center for Learning.

Math:

Biggs, E. 1970. *Freedom to learn.* Reading, Massachusetts: Addison-Wesley.
Burns, Marilyn. 1975. *The I hate mathematics book.* Boston: Little, Brown.
The Nuffield mathematics series. 1970. New York: John Wiley and Sons.

Human Processing Skills:

Boeke, Kees. 1957. *Cosmic view: the universe in 40 jumps.*
New York: John Day. (spatial orientation)
DeMille, Robert. 1967. *Put your mother on the ceiling.*
New York: Walker and Company. (mental imagery)
Fluegelman, Andrew. 1976. *The new games book.* Garden
City, New York: Doubleday. (gross motor)
Liepmann, Lise. 1973. *Your child's sensory world.* New
York: The Dial Press.
MacDonald Educational. 1976. *Ourselves.* London: Mac-
Donald Educational. (body image)
McKim, Robert. 1972. *Experiences in visual thinking.*
Monterey, California: Brooks-Cole.

Practical Life Skills:

Barratta-Lorton, Mary. 1972. *Workjobs.* Reading, Massachu-
setts: Addison-Wesley. (early childhood)
Campbell, David. 1974. *If you don't know where you're
going you'll probably end up somewhere else.* Niles:
Illinois: Argus Communications. (vocational)
Hollander, Annette. 1982. *How to help your child have a
spiritual life.* New York: Bantam.
Morrison, Eleanor S. and Price, Mila Underhille. 1974.
*Values in sexuality: a new approach to sex educa-
tion.* New York: Hart Publishing.
Wurman, Saul. 1973. *Yellow pages of learning resources.*
Cambridge, Massachusetts: MIT Press.

Behavioral/Affective/Social Skills

Briggs, Dorothy Corkille. 1970. *Your child's self-esteem.*
Garden City, New York: Doubleday.
Buzan, Tony. 1976. *Use both sides of your brain.* New
York: E. P. Dutton.
Canfield, Jack and Wells, Harold. 1976. *100 ways to im-
prove self-esteem in the classroom.* Englewood Cliffs,
New Jersey: Prentice-Hall.
Hendricks, Gay and Wills, Russell. 1975. *The centering
book: awareness activities for children, parents, and
teachers.* Englewood Cliffs, New Jersey: Prentice-Hall.

Oaklander, Violet. 1978. *Windows to our children.* Moab, Utah: Real People Press.

Vitale, Barbara Meister. 1982. *Unicorns are real: a right-brained approach to learning.* Rolling Hills Estate, California: Jalmar Press.

Weinstein, Matt and Goodman, Joel. 1980. *Playfair: everybody's guide to noncompetitive play.* San Luis Obispo, California: Impact.

Content/Knowledge Skills:

Blake, J. and Ernst, B. 1976. *The great perpetual learning machine.* Boston: Little, Brown.

Educational Development Center. 1971. *A working guide to the elementary science study.* Newton, Massachusetts.

Schrank, Jeffrey. 1972. *Teaching human beings: 101 subversive activities for the classroom.* Boston: Beacon Press.

Child Development

Elkind, David. 1981. *The hurried child: growing up too fast too soon.* Reading, Massachusetts: Addison-Wesley.

LeShan, Eda. 1968. *The conspiracy against childhood.* New York: Atheneum.

Montessori, Maria. 1973. *The secret of childhood.* New York: Ballantine.

Moore, Raymond S. and Moore, Dorothy N. 1977. *Better late than early.* New York: Reader's Digest Press.

Neumann, Erich. 1973. *The child.* New York: Harper and Row.

Pearce, Joseph Chilton. 1977. *Magical child.* New York: E. P. Dutton.

Piaget, Jean. 1951. *The child's conception of the world.* London: Humanitas Press.

Steiner, Rudolf. 1970. *Education as an art.* Blauvelt, New York: Rudolf Steiner Publications.

Wickes, Frances. 1968. *The inner world of childhood.* New York: New American Library.

Personal Growth and the Teacher

Assagioli, Roberto. 1965. *Psychosynthesis.* New York: Viking.

Jersild, Arthur T. 1955. *When teachers face themselves.* New York: Teachers College Press.

Progoff, Ira. 1975. *At a journal workshop.* New York: Dialogue House Library.

Truch, Stephen. 1980. *Teacher burnout and what to do about it.* Novato, California: Academic Therapy Publications.

Teacher-Student Interaction

Dennison, George. 1969. *The lives of children.* New York: Random House.

Herndon, James. 1969. *The way it spozed to be.* New York: Bantam.

Kohl, Herb. 1967. *36 children.* New York: Signet.

Lederman, Janet. 1979. *Anger and the rocking chair.* New York: McGraw-Hill.

Additional Resources

Clearinghouses in special education:

ERIC Clearinghouse on Exceptional Children
1920 Association Drive
Reston, Virginia 22091

NICEM—National Information Center for
    Educational Media
University of Southern California
University Park
Los Angeles, California 90007

Suppliers of Educational Resources

(tests, instructional materials, books, media, etc.)

Academic Therapy Publications
20 Commercial Boulevard
Novato, California 94947

Addison-Wesley Publishing
2725 Sand Hill Road
Menlo Park, California 94025
(innovative teaching methods)

American Guidance Service
Publishers' Building
Circle Pines, Minnesota 55014
(testing, instructional kits)

Anthroposophic Press
Threefold Farm
Hungry Hollow Road
Spring Valley, New York 10977
(integrated arts approach to special education)

Argus Communications
7440 Natchez Avenue
Niles, Illinois 60648
(self-concept/affective/interpersonal)

Children's Book and Music Center
5373 West Pico Boulevard
Los Angeles, California 90019

Creative Playthings
Princeton, New Jersey 08540
(perceptual/sensory-motor)

Creative Publications
3977 East Bayshore Road
Box 10328
Palo Alto, California 94303
(math/cognitive)

Edmund Scientific
101 East Gloucester Pike
Barrington, New Jersey 08007
(behavioral/perceptual/scientific)

Galt Toys
63 Whitfield Street
Guilford, Connecticut 06437
(concrete manipulatives)

Instructo/McGraw Hill
Cedar Hollow Road
Paoli, Pennsylvania 91301

Lakeshore Curriculum Materials
16463 Phoebe Street
La Mirada, California 90637

Nienhuis-Montessori USA
320 Pioneer Way
Mountain View, California 94040

Pitman Learning Inc.
6 Davis Drive
Belmont, California 94022
(academic content/basic skills, class management)

The Psychological Corporation
757 Third Avenue
New York, New York 10017
(formal assessment)

Special Child Publications
Box 33548
Seattle, Washington 98133
(educational tests, programs, and books)

Synectics Educational Systems
121 Brattle Street
Cambridge, Massachusetts 02138
(creativity/cognitive styles)

Uniquity
412 C Street
Galt, California 95632
(affective/self-concept books, materials, equipment)

Western Psychological Services
12031 Wilshire Boulevard
Los Angeles, California 90025
(formal assessment)

Whole Earth Catalogue
Box 428
Sausalito, California 94966
(practical life equipment)

The Author

Thomas Armstrong received a Master's degree in Special Education (learning disabilities) from Lesley Graduate School of Education in 1976. He worked as a learning disabilities specialist for five years in public and parochial schools in Canada and California. He is presently director of Latebloomers Educational Consulting Services (P. O. Box 2647, Berkeley, California) and teaches childhood and adolescent development at John F. Kennedy University, Orinda, California, while pursuing doctoral studies in psychology at the California Institute of Integral Studies, San Francisco, California.